AF483241

Perfectionism

An Imperfect Musing on The Shame of NOT Being a Magician Who Could Do the Impossible

Loran Joly

ReEnvision Press

Contents

Chapter One

Are We Fussing Over Details?

It would appear that we tend to view perfectionism as both a "Fussing over details", endlessly.

And secondly, in terms of, "If I DON'T do this or that 'PERFECTLY', I will 'catch heck'."

Chapter Two

Are We Afraid of BEING a "PERFECTIONIST", and so we DON'T DO MUCH at ALL?

But surely we can also SELF-IMPOSE a FALSE idea, in which we tell ourselves, “Don’t even *TRY* to MAKE THINGS any BETTER than just 'throwing something together'”, as if “Rough Draft = Final Copy”.

"AFTER ALL, You DON’T WANT to BE a ‘PERFECTIONIST’, Do You?”

Or, we may take on the view that any and all efforts - any Projects - are said by ourselves to be "DONE", when they are “80% done”, as per the phrase, “80% = Done”.

***

But then, would we find it very enjoyable to watch top athletes who had stopped improving their craft when they deemed themselves to have reached an "80%" level, and who then told themselves, "This is it: 80% is DONE, and so I'm moving in, in life"?

No! Top athletes, top performers, in general, are surely CRAFTING their Craft, "Honing" things:

Subject to whatever views they happen to have, regarding The Best "Life Balance" they come up with.

Chapter Three

Regarding the phrase "You're OBSESSING over DETAILS..."

Now, some also may think of the phrase, though, of "He or she is OBSESSING over their pursuit, their Craft, their efforts."

But what does this mean?

***

For what if the word "OBSESSING" simply refers to the AMOUNT of *TIME* we are putting in, compared to most others?

Or what we are giving up, to pursue this interest?

Or perhaps, even, that someone is pursuing one area, but neglecting other areas, and so is becoming "LOPSIDED"?

Like the proverbial teenager who eats, sleeps, and breathes one thing only, such as snowboarding, swimming, dating, or what have you?

CHAPTER FOUR

Freud's PLEASURE Principle

It strikes me, that we might invoke Freud's Pleasure Principle, that we are, as humans, motivated both to GAIN PLEASURE, and to AVOID PAIN.

> "The pleasure principle suggests we are motivated to obtain pleasure and avoid pain. Sometimes referred to as the pleasure-pain principle, this motivating force helps drive behavior, but it also wants instant satisfaction."
>
> https://www.verywellmind.com/what-is-the-pleasure-principle-2795472

***

And what might we be MOST seeking to AVOID, as per pain?

Perhaps, it not PAIN, physically or emotionally, PER SAY, which we seek to AVOID, but rather, how we are INTERPRETING this pain:

***

Are we SEEING (framing) the "pain" as a CATASTROPHE, or a matter of something simply being UNCOMFORTABLE?

***

And once we look at all events and how we FEEL, in turn, in this way, we might next ask, "*WHAT* do we MOST TEND to CATASTROPHIZE?"

Chapter Five

What are we AFRAID of the MOST?

What are we CASTROPHIZING the MOST?

Some say, that what drives many of us "bonkers", is UN-PREDICTABILITY".

And so, that we may catastrophize, in turn, UNPREDICTABILITY.

***

But what if this, while true, needs further explaining?

What if, say, we most fear, we most CATASTROPHIZE, is the **UNPREDICTABILITY of FEELING SHAME?**

And in turn, we find it VERY SHAME-inducing, to BE IMPERFECT?

To be IMPERFECT in some particular area:

and to HAVE THIS POINTED OUT to us, in turn.

Chapter Six

Are we Afraid of SHAME the MOST?

So, to dive still further, might we say that WHAT GENERATES SHAME, in turn, is a notion that WE *COULD* - *somehow* - have DONE OTHER than WHAT we DID do?

***

Hence, we may think, in our mind, phrases such as:

> **"SHAME on you for BEING IMPERFECT - for NOT having 'done' something or other PERFECTLY!"**

As if we were MAGICIANS who seemingly can CREATE SOMETHING out of NOTHING, out of "THIN AIR"...

That we can DEFY the Laws of the Universe, and then in turn, Bake a Cake without ALL the necessary INGREDIENTS; and without the PROPER overall external ENVIRONMENT, too. (Without the oven itself, say....)

***

21.

So, some of us, it appears, are told, either by one or both of our parents or others in our society, growing up, phrases such as:

> **"SHAME on you, for DOING this or that IMPERFECTLY: for NOT ACCOMPLISHING the IMPOSSIBLE, all things considered:"**

For, “DON’T you KNOW, that ‘WHERE there’s a WILL, there’s a WAY?"

***

And so, “YOU must be either ‘LAZY’; or, ‘you DIDN’T ‘TRY hard enough’”; or, “You DROPPED the BALL”; or, “You are simply a ‘BAD PERSON’”; or, “You thought you could ‘GET OVER on me' and others, didn’t you?”; or, “You are ‘IRRESPONSIBLE’”; or, “YOU are an ADDICT”; or, “You are simply ‘SELFISH” and “JUST DON’T CARE about ANY-ONE or anything BUT YOURSELF”.

CHAPTER SEVEN

Why Might a Parent be a "SHAMER" and thus induce "PERFECTIONISM" in a Child?

Now WHY WOULD a parent "DO" such "to" a child?

Several thoughts come to my mind:

For one thing, the parent may be TRYING to garner **VALIDATION** that THEY THEIRSELVES are Omnipotent and can thus ACCOMPLISH the IMPOSSIBLE:

This IMPOSSIBLE, being "perfection": without all the necessary INGREDIENTS, to boot.

Or the parent may be JEALOUS (aka "envious"), that the CHILD may not NEED to BE concerned with SEEKING Omnipotency, so as TO feel SAFER.

***

Or, the parent may be trying, unconsciously, to BLAMESHIFT onto the CHILD, some or more of the REASONS WHY the parent CANNOT ADEQUATELY PROVIDE an OPTIMAL UPBRINGING, either as to their own CONCEPTS about Reality...

Or perhaps in terms of FINANCIAL resources, also.

And finally, what they may not be able to PROVIDE as per an OPTIMAL EXTERNAL ENVIRONMENT to LIVE in, overall, as per the NEIGHBORHOOD, school setting, and so on.

***

So, "I cannot FIX this, but cannot admit it to myself, and so, I am going to blameshift onto you, the difficulties you are experiencing...."

Chapter Eight

If Not Perfection, then WHAT MIGHT We Want to Pursue Instead?

Now, if we are not seeking PERFECTION, then WHAT *MIGHT* we WANT to pursue?

Perhaps we might best pursue GROWTH:

Or, if growing is not possible, because we have some impediment such as cancer, say, we in turn accomplish "acceptance" that growth at this point is not possible, perhaps.

***

It thus being very important – even CRUCIAL – to say, to ourselves, that PERFECTION can NEVER be ACHIEVED.

And that THIS is OK: this is to be HUMAN.

***

Perhaps, then, this phrase saying a whole lot:

> **That "We ALL DO the “BEST we CAN”, given what we are ‘HANDED’”, at any particular time.**

And then, we can feel at ease in pursuing GROWTH, RATHER than pursuing the AVOIDANCE of PAIN: in particular, the pain of feeling shame over what we simply CANNOT possibly DO.

Rather than "chastizing" ourselves, aka "Beating ourselves up", aka "Shaming ourselves".

Chapter Nine

Parents Can Only Do the Best They Can, Given the Resources at Hand

Yes, INSTEAD of the parent CONCEDING, at least TO THEMSELVES, that they are somewhat UN-EQUIPPED to OPTIMALLY RAISE the child", the message they may tell themselves is,

> **"YOU are FAILING to MAKE UP for the lack of resources at hand, by your FAILING to BE a MAGICIAN, so that, in turn, you WOULD be HAPPIER in life, as a result":**
>
> **aka, "YOU are BEING IMPERFECT!"**

So, the END RESULT?

"BE a MAGICIAN! Be PERFECT! Because I CAN'T!"

Chapter Ten

Iterative Growth

My experience is that if we are able to turn to seeking GROWTH instead of AVOIDING the PAIN of FEELING SHAME over NOT being able to DO the IMPOSSIBLE, we in turn can also then pursue what some refer to as MAKING IMPROVEMENTS; or, "ITERATIVE" improving of some "area"....

To re-emphasize:

Whereupon we SEEK to MAKE CONSTANT IMPROVEMENTS - if POSSIBLE - for the PLEASURE of it all -

RATHER than SEEKING to REACH PERFECTION, to seemingly AVOID PAIN.

Again, as per Freud's "PLEASURE Principle":

Or, as I might tweak,

Living a life of pursuing "PLEASURE", instead of pursuing a life of "AVOIDING (seeming) CATASTROPHES".

To my parents, who made this possible.

For instance, my mother, an immigrant from eastern Poland, having come to America at the age of twelve, after a two-week long boat journey, to Ellis Island....

My mother as a young gal in Europe, before coming to America

And to my father, too, a most astute Trainer in life....

Brought up in the ghettos of Philadelphia; left school at the age of seventeen; and later acquiring a GED and going on to obtain a Ph.D. degree at a major University in English Literature; who thus led to my interest and pursuit of writing at a very early age; and too, with respect to his love of photography, which also rubbed off on me.

Hence, "The apple doesn't fall far from the tree"?

Training!

Then, too, my grandparents:

For significantly, my grandmother raised me during my first four years, in my waking hours. And her husband – my grandfather – worked in the tool and die industry for cars; she was born in eastern Poland, like my mother, and was a farmer there; he was born in Odessa, Ukraine, and a Mennonite, and herb-collector and maker of many grandfather clocks in his spare time, on their farm in Michigan:

Grandparents in Niagara Falls

And to my farm experience, as a youth, each summer, in Michigan:

My great-grandmother, and my mother, and I, when I was seven or so, on my grandparent's farm

Then, too, to a man of great impact upon myself, too, from the ages of twelve to fourteen, starting when I first sought him out to help me obtain a ham radio license at that age of twelve:

Mr. Foster; who interestingly did have a foster child he raised when I knew him; he helped me obtain my ham license; he hunted; he took me to ham conventions and camped with me; he collected stamps and coins; and let me build electronic projects in his workshop; and even took me for a ride on his motorcycle, popping a wheelie

And finally, to "Religion":

Again, that of my grandmother, a Baptist; and my grandfather, a Mennonite from Ukraine - born in the city of Odessa.

The ethnic Baptist church I attended in the summers, when a youth, while on the farm the other six days of the week... German was spoken....

And to my parents' religious influence upon myself, too: for they almost became missionaries in the Plymouth Brethren Church – a group similar to the Amish, Mennonites, and Quakers: they were to be posted to Canada.

And to L'abri, started by Francis Schaeffer. Where I spent a week in training, at the Massachusetts branch, in 1982.

And later, other faiths, too....

Including the faith of the Native American Indians, whom I first came into contact with when living in California, having spent time exploring Arizona; and too, in Cherokee, North Carolina, and Vonure, Tennessee:

A photograph I made while visiting the Cherokee Indian Reservation in 2021, camping nearby for four days in a tent, in the Blue Ridge Mountains

I made a visit to Vonure, Tennessee, in 2021, to learn more about the Cherokee Indians. Amongst the sights was the Sequoya Birthplace Museum, featuring Sequoya, who had single-handedly created the Cherokee alphabet, under great duress. I again camped, this time in the Cherokee National Park near Vonure, for several days

About the Author

The author resides in Kentucky,

and welcomes comments at message@goldpogo.com

Key aspects of the author's life have included...

Last day at West Point in 1983

Author, left; aunt - middle, who was key to my growing by telling me I needed to get into therapy .. she lived in Beverly Hills and was in the entertainment industry, so a year later, I did .. psychoanalysis, with a physician at a local medical school in Kentucky, and continuing on a year later, with another physician, in San Diego, California; and cousin, right, in California, a few years after my time in the Army in Germany

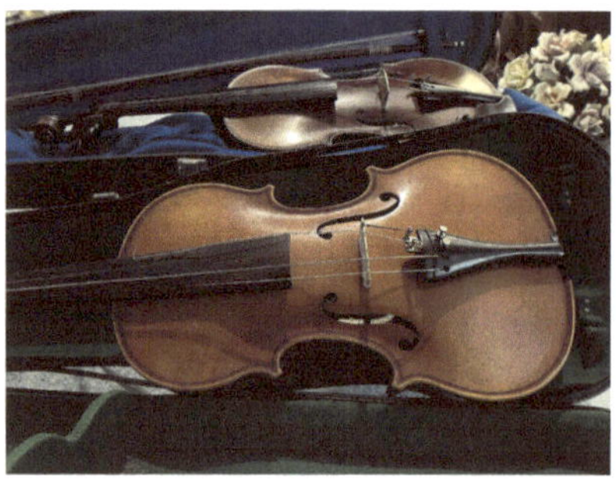

My violins: the closest one was purchased and carried on my father's back as he travelled in Germany. I started Suzuki violin lessons in North Carolina at the age of seven, and later studied at The MacPhail Center For Music in Minneapolis, Minnesota, when our family moved there in 1970 when I was ten; in eleventh grade, I played in a local college orchestra, and in my senior year, I took violin lessons at the University of Kentucky from a violin professor, and played in the Central Kentucky Youth Symphony Orchestra.

Where I spent three years' time writing, doing photography, and reading, and talking with the Wise Men of this village area on the Mississippi river in western Illinois, having no car, and coming by Greyhound with two large canvas bags of clothing, and hitchhiking the five miles from the Greyhound drop-off spot to this village of 800

One of many photographs I made while living for three years in Europe, around age 24

Another of my photographs made while living in Europe

A photograph I made while living in Europe, of a youth in England or Scotland

A photograph I made while living in Europe, perhaps at The Isle of Skye, in northernmost Scotland.

Berea College grounds, where I was the Ponderer of the Math department, studying only mathematics at the ages of forty-one through forty-five, and tutoring for the Berea College Mathematics Department, to pay off all my tuition at this scholarship-only college. Here I first learned to use a computer; and purchased my first cellphone: both at the young age of forty-one...

It was here that I continued my photography work, and including joining the local photo club, where I met a Mr. Warren Brunner, the town's portrait photographer, who I reconnected with in 2021 and was greatly encouraged by; he was instrumental in my future photo efforts, and a year after meeting with him frequently in 2021 and during 2022, I first started keeping a portfolio of images on Fine Art America's website; and then, started creating photo books on places in Kentucky; and then started a Shopify store in late 2022, too, to sell these.

One of many buildings at Berea College

Refund policy

Refund information:

If for any reason, you find this item not quite your cup of tea, I am most happy to provide a refund, no questions asked.

One can contact me at message@goldpogo.com.

Or, one can write me at this address, asking for a refund:

Loran Joly

Box # 1036

1303 US 127 South

Suite 104

Frankfort, KY 40601

www.ingramcontent.com/pod-product-compliance
Lightning Source LLC
Chambersburg PA
CBHW040746110726
47973CB00012B/193

* 9 7 9 8 3 3 0 3 1 7 6 7 7 *